MOTION STUDIES

ALSO BY BRAD RICHARD

Habitations
The Men in the Dark (chapbook)

Motion Studies

poems by BRAD RICHARD

WINNER OF THE
2010 WASHINGTON PRIZE

THE WORD WORKS
WASHINGTON, D.C.

FIRST EDITION   FIRST PRINTING
Motion Studies
Copyright © 2011 Brad Richard

Reproduction of any part of this book in any form or by any means, electronic or mechanical, except when quoted in part for the purpose of review, must be with permission from the publisher in writing. Address inquiries to:

The Word Works
PO Box 42164
Washington, DC 20015
wordworksbooks.org
editor@wordworksbooks.org

Cover art: *Swimming*, Thomas Eakins.
Used by permission, The Amon Carter Museum.
Author photograph: Christopher Jeansonne
Book design: Susan Pearce

Library of Congress Catalog Number: 2010933679
International Standard Book Number: 978-0-915380-78-7

The creative works contained herein are works of the imagination. Any resemblance to actual events, locales, or persons, living or dead, is entirely coincidental.

ACKNOWLEDGMENTS

Grateful acknowledgment is given to the editors of the journals in which some of these poems originally appeared:

Guernica: "Motion Studies" [series beginning "The worst part about driving in a storm . . ."] and "My Father's Studio."

Literary Imagination: "The Raft of the Medusa: after Théodore Géricault; *aux naufragés*."

Prairie Schooner: "Young Boy with Dead Crane—unidentified artist (no date)," "Masked Woman—unidentified artist (no date)," and "Dying Boy with Toys—unidentified artist (no date)" (as "From the Dark Chamber: Three Daguerreotypes").

Mississippi Review: "Fantasia on a Small Sketchbox for Thomas Eakins' *Swimming* (1885)" and "Background: *Swimming*, Thomas Eakins (1885)."

THERMOS: "*Fort-Da*."

ooooo

I owe a great debt of thanks to the staff of the Amon Carter Museum, Fort Worth, TX, for their invaluable research assistance on *Swimming* in the summer of 2004.

I am also deeply grateful to the Surdna Foundation and the Louisiana Division of the Arts for financial support for the research and writing of some of these poems, and to the Vermont Studio Center and the Ragdale Foundation for residencies that provided crucial time (and, at Ragdale in October, 2005, haven) for writing many of these poems.

Finally, I owe more thanks than I can convey to the many readers whose input helped shape my thinking on these poems and the problems they presented. Most especially: Dana Sonnenschein (steadfast, thoughtful, generous friend), Carolyn Hembree, Peter Cooley, Kay Murphy, Andy Young, Andy Stallings, Melissa Dickey, Elizabeth Thomas, Tonya Foster, Ed Skoog, Audrey Niffenegger, Tom Whalen. Never least, and sorely missed: Reginald Shepherd, without whose encouragement much of this book would not have come to be.

for Tim

CONTENTS

I.

From the Dark Chamber: Five Daguerreotypes	15
1. "Young Boy with Dead Crane"	15
2. "Masked Woman"	16
3. "Still Life with Pumpkin, Book, and Sweet Potato"	17
4. "Dying Boy with Toys"	18
5. "Big Mound During Destruction"	20
Motion Studies	22

II.

Background: *Swimming*, Thomas Eakins (1885)	29
Chronograph	30
The Artist's Wife and His Setter Dog, Thomas Eakins (1884-88)	31
Eakins Odalisque	32
Self-Portrait as Benjamin Fox: *Swimming*	35
Waterlines	37
Motion Studies	38

III.

Prelude to a Fantasia on a Small Sketchbox	45
Fantasia on a Small Sketchbox	46
Fort-Da	48
Three Essays on *Swimming*, Thomas Eakins (1885)	49
1. *Is it personal?*	49
2. *Is it democratic?*	53
3. *Is it natural?*	56
Susan Macdowell Eakins at the Memorial Exhibition of Her Husband's Work: Metropolitan Museum of Art, 1917	60

IV.

I Take a Book from the Shelf	66
The Raft of the Medusa: after Théodore Géricault; *aux naufragés*	68
Motion Studies	72
Barton Springs	80

NOTES	82
ABOUT THE AUTHOR	84
ABOUT THE WASHINGTON PRIZE	85
ABOUT THE WORD WORKS	86

... I am a primitive, a child—or a maniac; I dismiss all knowledge, all culture, I refuse to inherit anything from another eye than my own.

ROLAND BARTHES, *Camera Lucida*

I.

From the Dark Chamber: Five Daguerreotypes

Every object, however minute, is a perfect transcript of the thing itself... [W]ho knows whether, in this age of inventions and discoveries, we may not be called upon to marvel at the exhibition of a tree, a horse, or a ship produced by the human voice muttering over a metal plate... the words "tree," "horse," and "ship."

—*The Diary of Philip Hone,* December 4, 1839

When I began to take pictures... I had to make pictures of the dead.

—ALBERT S. SOUTHWORTH, "Comments at the National Photographic Association," 1873

1. "Young Boy with Dead Crane" —unidentified artist (ca. 1850)

He holds death close to his body,
the neck's curve limp in his fist, the wings
splayed like broken fans, the beak empty,
a stilled syllable. If it could stand,

its height from black claw to white crest
would clear the crown of the boy's hat,
and its wings, spread for flight, would span
wider than his reach if he were a man.

He has been brushed, preened, and posed
for this occasion, told he looks handsome,
told to hold still and be taken. Never

will I let go, he says. Look: this bird,
more beautiful than me, is weak, and I,
a boy, stronger. Death: why should I grow?

2. "Masked Woman"
—unidentified artist, no date

Behind the mask
lies a face.

A bonnet covers the head,
its curves cupping, beside each ear,

coiled dark curls, dense orbs.
There are frills, but the mask,

though pink, is plain, smooth
as imagined skin. Holes

show the eyes, the eyes,
you think, of a woman.

But what if the face
is only a scaffold

for the mask? Or
itself a mask? Or

what if the mask masks
the face of a man

masked as a woman
masked? Dark coils,

eyes that tell you
you can't imagine.

3. "Still Life with Pumpkin, Book, and Sweet Potato"
   —unidentified artist, no date

Hopeful, you set out a table
and whisper: *come forth, invisibles*.
And the invisibles oblige.

Pumpkin, book, and sweet potato
arrange themselves as if this world
were their idea as much as yours.

Voilá. That's all. They can't stay long,
but your invitation charmed them so.
Won't you join them, just for a moment,

and let them take you where they came from?
They've a place there just for you—
listen, someone is calling your name.

4. "Dying Boy with Toys"
     —unidentified artist, no date

A man comes to visit, carrying a funny toy:
a box with legs that slide out, and a black blanket
where he hides his head. *What's in the box?*

asks the boy. The man sits him up in bed to peek
through the hole, where the boy finds his mother
hunched over her sewing, sitting alone in a window

that only opens in the box. *How come you're here?*
To take your picture. *Yes, but why?* Your mother
wants something to keep. The boy nods: the man

didn't lie, the man looks sad. *Let's play.* All right.
Here? *No, in the parlor.* The man lifts the boy: light
as a ball, a pillow, a picture, a ghost of the weight

of grown bodies the man has tilted, turning their heads
over basins to spill their useless fluids. This small hand
kisses his neck, not the clumsy caress of a dead limb

whose resistant body he's embraced to set upright,
then forcing joints to bend so they fold again naturally.
Trembling, he sets the boy on a sofa, a taint of metal

haunting his mouth, blood-tinged bile rising in his throat:
mercury, he's used to it. *Do you like your work?*
asks the mother, who's followed them. He glances

at her busy hands, watches her pricking her thumb
with the bright needle, drawing tiny tears of blood.
Yes, he lies. The boy's head sags on the sofa's arm.

His mother stares. *He gets tired.* Does he have toys?
She shakes her head. *When his daddy got real sick,
we sold them.* She holds the needle in her thumbtip,

pushes harder. She sees him watching. *If you don't mind,
I'll be in the kitchen.* Apparatus moved from the boy's room,
distance judged, glass plate set, the man slips his head

into the dark to look, but a tremor in the image turns
boy to blurred shadow. He shuts his eyes, swallows,
looks again: the boy smiles, calls him to the window. *I want

a blue wagon,* he whispers in the man's ear. That's easy;
what else? *A white horse with a red saddle. And a swan,
a white swan. And a red drum.* I can do that, let me go

and I'll do it. The boy holds him harder. *All my toys.
All my toys, always. And don't tell mommy, but I want
my daddy's black silk hat.* The man shuts his eyes again,

opens them: it's all there, perfectly composed. Looks again:
what's in the box? A boy slumped in that empty window,
his mother shaking him. He shuts his eyes. Looks again.

5. "Big Mound During Destruction"
—Thomas Easterly (1869)

You who composed the image of this moment,
whatever it was you wanted me to see,

I can't. Yes, there are three workers,
pausing to pose with their spotted dog

on the mound's level top, their horses idle
by the dray, tired from hauling earth and trees.

And wheels have worked ruts in the slopes,
the ruts muddy from the scrawny rain

crawling across the scene, over the spectators
gathered at the base. But what that mound

meant that moment is lost. You must have taken
most of a morning to set up, more than a minute

to fix the image to the plate. Here, in ten
twinned seconds, a million and a half tons

of towered glass, concrete and steel collapsed,
blasted past belief. Time died. The wrecked

girders looked for a while like an enormous animal's ribs,
a cage for wind and dust and smoke from cindered bodies—

In your picture, one spectator, a man,
has removed his hat and turned his head

to look back at the camera, his glance alien
as it catches mine through the rain falling

across these low green mountains, the clouds
swallowing now one, then another, like hope.

Johnson, Vermont, 2002; New Orleans, 2009

Motion Studies

> *And it is all one to me*
> *Where I am to begin; for I shall return there again.*
>
> —PARMENIDES, *On Nature*

The Paradox: 1

According to Zeno,
        Achilles always fails
                to pass the tortoise:

kicking up dust breaking down
        into infinitely finer dust,
                his battle-calloused soles

bleed, and dust silts his throat
        and clots his sight, a cloud
                swelling and dividing

as it swallows the hero.
        A child could save him
                with a little math—*Look, mister,*

the numbers say you win—
        but once he starts, he knows
                this is the only story that matters,

as he knows the story fails him
        every time, as every story fails,
                and he wants to tell someone

but no matter how he runs
        he can't make it in time,
                at least, not this time, not yet—

Concerning Achilles

It takes a great hero to race a tortoise and lose.

    Achilles spurned by Troilus, Achilles sulking on the beach, Achilles grieving, Achilles dragging Hector's corpse, Achilles murdered by the coward Paris—why, he wonders now, as the race begins anew on another perfect morning, why did they ever matter? He doesn't need them. He doesn't need anyone.

    He is necessary, Achilles understands each time the race begins, as proof of a universal lack of necessity.

❦

Achilles, in Hades, has just opened his mouth to tell Odysseus that he would sooner be a live slave than king of the dead, when he awakes and remembers: I'm not dead, it's time for the race. But as he ties back his hair, he wonders: which Achilles am I? Myself or my ghost? Or the dream of one of my ghosts?

❦

The tortoise, generally and almost exclusively an herbivore, is nonetheless tempted by a grub whose burrow lies just below the surface of the track.

The Paradox: 2

According to Zeno,
>> time is composed of instants too small
>>>> and dense to divide. Thus, no body

can be in one place at an instant's start
>> and another at its end. Thus, an arrow
>>>> must already have pierced the spleen

and scraped the ribs of its howling target,
>> and disturbed a newborn blowfly's flight
>>>> with its trembling bronze tip riving, raveling

the indivisible if, once sprung from its bow,
>> it flies. Thus, motion is impossible,
>>>> and change, illusion. Everything stays

exactly as it is, the tortoise
>> nosing out a grub from the dirt,
>>>> Achilles running in place in his static cloud...

Concerning Zeno

Zeno was *eromenos* to his teacher, Parmenides. To help his teacher prove the immutability and indivisibility of all things-that-are, he came up with several paradoxes that brought his *erastes* to philosophical tears of joy. Zeno's fame lives on to this day.

※

At some point, in some accounts, Zeno and his friends were involved in a plot to overthrow a tyrant. Zeno was captured and brought before the tyrant, who demanded the names of the conspirators. Zeno named all the tyrant's friends. Pressed to say if there were others, Zeno said, "Yes, you are the pestilence destroying the city!" Then

—he said he needed to whisper something in the tyrant's ear, leaned in close, and

> bit him and wouldn't let go until stabbed.
> bit his nose off.
> stabbed the tyrant.

—turning to the bystanders, he called them cowards and bit off his own tongue, which he spat at the tyrant, thus inciting the crowd to stone their tormentor to death.

—for his insolence, and to set an example, the tyrant put Zeno in a mortar and had him pounded and hacked to pulp and pieces. Zeno became not-Zeno.

※

Zeno lived on and on, as if unchanging. Finally, at the age of ninety-eight, he strangled himself.

The Paradox: 3

Once, twice, or *n* upon a time,
    there are two parallel lines,
        one called *Arrow*, the other *Achilles*.

For *n* years, they remain apart
    and cannot change and cannot move.
        One day, long after Zeno + not-Zeno = 1,

Arrow and *Achilles* bend in their flight
    to a point, a solitude of the void,
        before their stories begin, where they converge

and end in one another: *Arrow* and *not-Achilles*,
    Achilles and *not-Arrow*, *not-Achilles*
        and *not-Arrow*, *Achilles* and *Arrow*

are one. Meanwhile, the tortoise
    scoops the grub into its beak
        and pulls itself down the road.

❦

Once upon a time

Achilles begins, out of breath, arriving as he meets the arrow.

    Riven, raveled, he'll never make it in time.

II.

Background: *Swimming,* Thomas Eakins (1885)

Call it green-beyond-the-bodies
of men naked one gilded afternoon
at Dove Lake, at the foundation
of this abandoned mill, call it

green not imagining green,
forest that is no forest,
green whose edges articulate
eidetic forms of branch and leaf,

green whose first body burned,
born ultra-basic in magma's
coolings, hardest crystals,
aspectral green, unseen as mined

until purged from not-green,
worked free from coarse metal,
call it viridian, oxide of chromium,
dark matter against which these bodies

stand, recline or dive in time
into bearable elements, bodies
of weight or light or mind,
or not bodies, paint layered

as light as flesh, layer
bearing layer into light,
of course labored, not the work
of these nudes who study green

leisure reflected in the image
of water they reach toward, water
pushing forth their images, shades
at the bare stone base of this mill.

Chronograph

Four figures trace
        one body's actions framed
                by we who study time:

            stand

      rise
                dive

    climb

All summer staging boys at play
        on rocks, in water through my lens,
                I modeled in my mind one motion,

held all winter inside me
        one body dissected as four,
                until, the site fixed to canvas,

I rendered each figure from life,
      meat to bone.
               Scholar, let no body

unthink his passage, decompose my thought,
        the standing boy bend, or the diver
                sink through his reflection's curve.

And where their motion shatters
        on the river's wrinkled face,
                let my image swim against decay.

The Artist's Wife and His Setter Dog, Thomas Eakins (1884-88)

Just look at her, slumped in her chair,
one hand limp on those prints in her lap,
the fingers curled, cringing from light
brutal as a surgeon's lamp—see, it flays
every fold of her dress, hollows her chest,
smears shadows on her neck and cheek. I can't
imagine who would care to touch her.

This dog on the rug, though—
don't you want to coo in his ears
and rub his belly? *Good dog,* you'd say,
and it's true, this dog is faithful
to his image, warm and friendly,
russet coat redolent of grass and streams.
Even the wife can almost smell it.

Her lips start to smile, then stop as she hides
behind her eyes, those flat black disks
he fixed in her sockets as he scraped and daubed,
undoing her face. Everyone looks and says
She might as well be dead. I hardly know
the difference now, it's been that long since I felt
his wet brush stroking me out of my skin.

Eakins Odalisque

after a photograph of Thomas Eakins, ca. 1883

He's posed himself, a nude, middle-aged man, reclining like an odalisque, the lowest harem woman, on a dingy couch in a dim attic. His back's to us, his head bent, half-turned, half-shadow. Someone—student? maybe wife—helped him take the picture.

1. **Anatomy**

                        Propped on your stiff left arm,

          legs stretched out, slightly bent,
              you're tricked so

we double-take,
        seeing your big, shadow-cleft bottom,

                contrivance of light and weight

to bear this body
        desiring to bear
                this body desiring—

2. *Différance*

Forged and espoused in his pose,
        the *Grande Odalisque*, the *Olympia*,
                imperious slaves. From their several divans,

the harem women stare, dare us not to look:
        more than their makers, those masters, they know
                our desires. His? Apprenticed to such arts, he looks

away,

                leaves us wanting—

3. The attic (after)

Clothed in its own

No trace, stain, scent

Otherwise neglected space

Workplace and storage

Take note as I remove this

Not far from the academy

"Community: Nudity and Fantasy"

And here's his wife, nude beside a horse, her face scratched out

Self-Portrait as Benjamin Fox: *Swimming*

Soon—but first
I bend to stir
my face in the water

slurred hurry of my floating red hair
my hand down in it past the wrist
past all worry of *I was*

Soon—but now
my other hand grips
a cleft in the rock ledge

a little darkness enough
to steady my stir and hurry
not bind my bending here

Soon—but why
am I this body
if this image

pulls me to light and dark
depths of what hand
worries all away

Soon—then let
no stroke nor stir
unsteady me

churn my floating head
no hand inside me bend
image into being

Soon—little
darkness—hold
past I was

Waterlines

I tried and failed to read the flood's trace data,
        to track its shifting levels, sinking mostly,
scumming walls, trees, a bread truck, fences,
        striae of engine oil, lake muck, waste and rust,

like flatlines like cross-cut strata like shear
        of mountainside freeway-gouged, no, like nothing
but neighborhoods' bulldozer-mounded strew
        of gutted things slopped, toxic, hauled to landfill,

oh memory, fuck if I know
        what I came home to, expecting what
ransack, salvage, matter to claim, name
        for isn't and everywhere.

Motion Studies

1. [My father's studio, 2005]

As if browsing in a gallery,
    I flip through canvases leaning against the wall
        behind my father's studio. A clear October day,

the air breezeless, birdless. Silence
    still cloys like oily mud, two months
        since the flood. The studio's siding sags;

the back door won't close. I look in:
    heaps of clothes rotting, shelves of LPs,
        their jackets fused, some swollen books,

and, further back in muck and shadow,
    forty years of work my father made,
        and catalogues, and slides, and reviews.

I step back into the sunlight,
    look through the canvases again,
        remember my father working on them,

and time unravels and I see myself
    doing the things a ghost does,
        shuffling inside the narrow frame

of a world of ruined images. Yes,
    I remember these paintings.
        They were good. And I remind myself:

he's already repainting them.
    They're still good.
        Stop acting like a ghost.

2. [My grandmother's bed, ca. 1972]

I never knew my mama, *she tells me*
    again, a fingernail tapping my wrist,
        her satin pillowcase cool against my cheek.

No, I never did: she died—*all night, her fan*
    turns while she calls back her dead.
        Neurons twitch and snag. I listen, call her back:

no, she died having me. Later, my daddy
    married some other lady and gave me away,
        I didn't know why: I asked God: did I kill Mama?

The judge said, Mary, your aunt's adopting you,
    will you keep your daddy's name? No sir,
        I said, no I won't. My aunt's rooming house

was over on Proctor Street, all those people
    coming and going. *Her fingers grip mine,*
        now loose, now tighter, the one nail

tapping, nervous step testing
    my skin for a bridge—
        bridge of canasta decks and pressed roses,

dollar bills she'd give me from her Bible,
    the pink clock's hum on her nightstand, flicker
        of its numbers, headlights blurred in rain—

When Paw Paw was a boy, one of his brothers died
    here in Port Arthur. The undertaker's telegram
        said he'd keep on ice till they came,

so Paw Paw and his daddy—they had an old truck—
      a hundred miles, and flooding all the way,
           roads washed out—it took two days—

tangled fibers of her neurons,
      proteins collapsing cell by cell—
           he was in the ground by the time they got here—

You know that white bird in that picture
      on my dresser? Your daddy painted that,
           you think he'd paint me another sometime

Did you call last night? Did you come visit?
      I saw my daddy sitting right there on the couch
           That boy on Proctor Street had a big mean dog

and I told him you leave me be
      Come help Maw Maw cut her hair tomorrow
           I can't do it anymore remember I showed you

that bird eating bread I threw in the yard
      well one day it ate right out of my hand
           like this:

3. [The cooling board, 1929]

He tried to ask someone what happened
    to the back of his head, but the words
        fell apart in his mouth and got caught

like stones in his throat, and he ended up here
    in his one good shirt and a friend's old suit.
        June, but it's cool where he is, laid out

on a woven cane mat stretched taut
    in a folding frame over a block of ice,
        the whole getup tented in silk.

But no one ever told him what happened,
    not his friends who carried him in,
        not the undertaker who slicked his hair

over the rut left by a steel rod that shot
    like an arrow when a gas still burst a pipe
        right when he was leaning in to check it—

the refinery's paying for the funeral.
    If you cared to look in his wallet,
        you'd find a pretty girl's picture

inscribed *for my "Spindletop,"* and another,
    clipped from the *Port Arthur News*, of a whale
        seventy feet long, beached at Sabine Pass—

that would have been a story to tell!
    The ice sweats a slow fever in its pan,
        and weird dew on his cheek makes runnels

through rice powder and rouge, and the words
    finally settle, down low in his windpipe.
        Would you believe he grew up on a rice farm

outside Gueydan? That he loved the smell of asphalt
    on his skin when he woke? Well, that's all over.
        But lift the drape and he'll tell you what it's like

now in his palace of jacquard and ice.

III.

Prelude to a Fantasia on a Small Sketchbox

(In the museum)

Cotton-gloved, the curator presents me the pieces:
>the box, smaller than I imagined, its frame's slats grooved for
>>three slim boards—or for two and the lid?
>
>the lid, its back a palette of three or four tones;
>on one side of the surviving board, a standing three-quarter
>>figure, on the other,
>
>a landscape in quick strokes and dabs.

No longer sure what I'm supposed to see, I scribble:

>*scabs of paint on the figure; the landscape's greens shiver.*

Hard to catch the tones in this light, she says. Let's open the blinds.

>*paste of rock, shadow, flesh*

Color notations, says the curator. Few details, and here the wood shows through the green.

>*paint's memory—a world before bodies?*

This figure, she says, isn't as confident as the finished one. Less sure of himself. Of course, these are just sketches; things change in process.

>*used, wounded, real*

Fantasia on a Small Sketchbox

SKETCH = BOX

Touch my broken story: brackets to slats grooved to hold boards to hold pigment, river to rock to hold warm to cold, then to now. Holding open. Holding shut. Held whole, a wooden book telling water telling boy. Broken still to tell bracket to slat to river to nude to hold.

PALETTESCAPE

Stroke and stir. Suppose green before anywhere grown. Repose of no body, white all morning is no event but what. Is red sun black memory. Is a whetting. My stroke and what stir.

FIGURE

To be is yet to be mastered.

LANDSKETCH

My planes are all one. What is solid is fixed flow. Gray-violet disposes sky to think meadow to forest to rock, think flesh yet untold. Green strokes a grassbank where my stream will away. Petals kindle out of shadow. Round flat flames. Or. And. Sentence for now sentience.

RE: FIGURE

Rose-streaked peach and shadow-belly boy, impasto impostor. Butter-lick and sunburn neck, no friends but green and blue. Such thick nothings. Still touching true.

PALETTESCAPE (INVERTED)

Green sets red to fall. No sky for my yellow star. Smear me lead and lampblack. Scar and no anthem.

BOX = X

Touch shuts my summer scene.

Fort-Da

Gone and there our bodies, near and not to hold. Here: forest to chromium, stone to umber, violet clouds the far water. Here: each of our bodies as one forgets, posed in difference. You derive from this, a gaze, a farther delayed, incomplete all ways. Eternal arrival where we never, our pleasure made gone, there, in our forest's grayed down greens, in our stream's graded hues, in use, in you. *I* never seen, tell us *naked*, tell us *heat* or *him*, tell us *touch*, tell *death* your story, our bodies, there, gone, each a child's toy, a reel he tosses past sight, *o-o-o-o*, pulls back by its thread. Thread we play you hold. *Here*:

Three Essays on Thomas Eakins' *Swimming* (1885)

1. *Is it personal?*

I'm twelve, wading with my mother
      in a stream, shorts held high
            above the water, my white briefs

sodden and sagging. Looking away,
      smiling, my mother says
            You might as well take those off.

They'll soak your shorts, she says,
      you'll just wet the car seat;
            she knows I want to be naked

as stream, limestone, scrub oak, hawk,
      another self among selves.
            I'm twelve, wading,

just naked enough now
      for you to see me as this *I*
            I can only imagine. Reader,

other: in our summer scene,
      the light warms my wet skin
            as if I've just been painted here.

ooooo

Touching rock, touching water,
        the six men of Eakins' painting
                inhabit their bodies exactly

as he imagined them, as he watched
        from the water, swam back to the rocks.
                All winter in his attic studio,

he has staged summer's bodies
        as if they were together
               at Mill Creek.

He is glad they are themselves,
        the models posed to screen from view
                genitalia and most of their faces,

disposes each not to touch
        the skin of any other, or to see
                what holds a companion's attention;

he molds a wax maquette of the diver;
        he scrapes, refigures, scrapes
                men and rock, retouches water.

Half-dissolved, his own image swims
        in the stream whose reflections
                are as fine as the hairs on his head.

⚬⚬⚬⚬⚬

Given over to their touch,
> I know them and myself in them.
>> I'm the look on the face of the journalist

reclining on the rock ledge; I say
> *You don't know what I'm thinking.*
>> Below him wades a red-haired boy, turned,

gripping the rocks—I'm his other hand
> searching the water; and the dirty feet
>> of the kneeling protégé who lifts one arm

as if teasing Harry, Eakins' setter;
> and the sunburned neck of the student
>> standing arms akimbo, backside to you;

and the inverted beard
> of the Union veteran diving
>> to join his reflection rising.

I'm the wet skin of Thomas Eakins
> and warmed by the sun I say
>> you don't know what I'm thinking.

ooooo

You might as well take those off—
        naked in clear light, clear water,
                cloud-shadow, hawk-shadow, I.

If the body pictured is figure,
        to be is yet to be mastered—
                Look: even as the diver's arms

break the water's surface
        where he meets his reflected eyes,
                his companions "are contrived

to gaze outside the picture
        that frames them. What do they see?"
                Never ourselves, looking in

on bodies we want to inhabit,
        ghosts in a drama of seeing
                our desires come close to nothing.

This thought suspends the diver
        the sky the rock the water
                suspends this knowledge of his skin.

2. *Is it democratic?*

Listen: you won't hear hammers slung on steel,
        or calls of stevedores at the docks;
                no bickering in market stalls,

the ragman's plaint, the newsboy's cry,
        trolley's bell, cop's whistle, screams
                of a child crushed by carriage wheels.

And no gunsmoke, no drumtaps:
        it's twenty years since the war.
                Here, the air is fresh, and no noise

distracts these men, these citizens,
        from bathing in freedom
                imagined at an abandoned mill.

Even the diver—George Reynolds,
        9th New York Cavalry Regiment,
                Congressional Medal of Honor

for taking Virginia's flag at Opequon—
        dives unheard, silence the anthem
                uniting these isolatoes.

ooooo

June 18, 1885: two hundred fourteen crates
    arrive at Bedloe Island in New York,
        Liberty as yet unassembled.

She'll stare across the Atlantic.
    Now watch as Jesse Godley turns
        his bright body away, face in shadow

as he calls our gaze to the picture plane
    and no farther, staring where the diver's
        body shatters shade and reflection.

Or will, soon enough: composed,
    so long as we look, their bodies'
        arc holds them in place, in a place

not paradise, not even home,
    barely natural, their freedom
        imagined in a place abandoned,

a place man-made, of layered rocks,
    the stream widened by a dam,
        the pigments ground and blended.

ooooo

"very democratic, but all decent behaving":
        Whitman, watching "squads of boys"
                bathing by the Harlem River,

"glittering drops sparkling," "the dark
        green shadow of the hills," boys laughing
                and diving, their "movements, postures,

ahead of any sculpture." Whitman watching,
        Whitman listening, democratizing,
                sits alone "under an old cedar

half way up the hill," believes his boys,
        "[a] peculiar and pretty carnival,"
                rehearse for him an art unknown,

figured in their live, loud bodies.
        Chaste motifs of an August day,
                echoes of the poet's artifice: as if touch

would connect us, would signify
        noble *kratos* and loving *demos*
                (akin to *daiomai*, "I divide").

3. *Is it natural?*

This is fullness: your body brightening,
        turned away. Jesse, the sky's heat,
                diffused in grass and water,

catches on your naked skin,
        on buttocks' slope and shoulder blades,
                on the tip of your right ear.

This is fullness unknown to you,
        bright boy posing on a rock
                at twenty-two. At twenty-three,

you betray your teacher, your creator;
        you "marry well" at twenty-five;
                at twenty-six, dead of typhus

and father of a newborn son.
        Turned away, your body bears
                the brief weight of this moment

with no need of any other,
        and a life's unsettled shadows
                are nothing to your nature now.

ooooo

In the locker room at the gym,
        I look at naked young men
                who don't look back, their art,

like yours, to exclude yet hold me
        watching, with them all summer.
                "I see no impropriety in looking

at the most beautiful of Nature's works,
        the naked figure" of this one
                and this one and this one.

Like you, they turn away, open lockers,
        slip into clothes and out the door.
                We are always here and gone,

in the showers' hiss, the AC's chill,
        or the breeze on sun-warmed skin,
                we are figures of one body, perhaps

beautiful, or not, proper or not.
        When I turn away, I take
                whatever filled my sight.

ooooo

Whitman returns, averring that "everything
    comes out of the dirt—everything;
        everything comes out of the people,

the everyday people, the people
    as you find them and leave them,"
        and we go back to dirt (or used to)

and the painter grinds the right dirts
    (or used to) and makes us believe
        these images of dirt are something

more or less every day.
    Every day I can find you
        on my computer screen, in pages

of several books on my shelves,
    even in a museum, should I choose
        to make the long drive back

to Fort Worth from New Orleans
    to see you on Dove Mill's rocks,
        rocks now built over in some suburb.

ooooo

You are fullness: imago brightening
 against the forest's deepening green.
  You might as well take those off,

my mother said as I waded in a stream,
 in the heat of Texas in July,
  and when I did, that nakedness

engendered others yet unknown.
 Call this one Jesse Godley, and these
  Benjamin Fox, Talcott Williams,

Laurie Wallace, George Reynolds,
 Thomas Eakins and his setter,
  Harry, swimming back to the rocks,

or a life's unsettled shadows . . .

Sun's going down; time to dress
 for the long ride home. We'll return
  in the fullness of other selves.

Susan Macdowell Eakins at the Memorial Exhibition of Her Husband's Work: Metropolitan Museum of Art, 1917

> *Mrs. Eakins was kinda killed when she married.*
> —A family friend, after SME's death.

[*The Gross Clinic*, 1875]

I studied; I married . . .

When I saw your painting of Dr. Gross
       in surgery, scalpel steady as a pen
              in bloody fingers, I didn't flinch.

At the Academy, you helped me dissect
       corpses to see form's roots, smiled
              when I tried to make a tendon twitch.

I studied, I married

your studio, your palette, the photographs
       of you naked with your students one summer
              at Dove Lake and the Jersey shore.

I was never one of your boys;
       my hand kept accounts, wrote letters,
              signed paintings for you after your death.

Widowed, I study

again these sixty canvases
       and think of Bobby, our pet monkey,
              whom Sam Murray begged you to shoot

after I suffered a second bite.
    I bandaged my hand, took my camera
        and laid the little fellow out.

ooooo

[*Singing a Pathetic Song*, 1881]

Dim in the background, I'm bent
    at the piano as the singer finishes.
        Eyes on the score, I should guide

the girl's voice, hold the last note
    at her lips. But I wasn't there
        when you posed Margaret in the attic

by an old piano seat, her only audience
    her handsome painter and her picture,
        turned away. She never sang

that I could hear. And I wasn't there
    at the Academy the day you lifted
        a model's loincloth to draw

your female students' eyes to nature.
    Even now, mine stay on the score,
        holding true to your design.

Stupid of them to have fired you
    over that nub of flesh. Stupid girl
        who never saw nor sang.

ooooo

[*Mrs. Thomas Eakins, ca. 1899*]

I see my hand in it—my eyes
        won't lift from you. Remember
                the photograph you took of me nude

beside a horse at Avondale farm?
        Someone has scratched out my face,
                with a nail file's tip, I think, perhaps

taken from my dressing table.
        Avondale: your poor niece, Ella,
                breaking out of her locked room

to steal the rifle from your studio
        and do herself in—could she have found
                that photo there, that afternoon?

Imagine my nail file in jealous fingers,
        like your brush in your own,
                and my eyes, never lifting—

[*Thomas Eakins, Self-Portrait, 1902*]

"I confess

I fear always the so-called, expert restorer,
    if the effort is not understood
        irreparable damage may be done . . ."

That's what I wrote to them,
    for all the good it may do.
        Relined, revarnished, reframed,

these pictures hold a while, hide their scars
    as years darken their glazes.
        Even the places my brush worked

to help your failing sight. Tom,
    I think I'd like to show myself
        in this drafty gallery, step away

from my loosened dress, reveal my body
    bare as rock and wrinkled water,
        dark wood and mottled sky,

unrestored. Poor Bobby; do you know,
    I still think of him every time
        you look on me as if I understand.

IV.

I Take a Book from the Shelf

Infinity and the Mind
              and shards of glass fall out

so I'm back in the tornado
       crouched with my husband
              and the dog in the hallway

while wind seizes the house
       shatters windows and rips
              the roof away   tarpaper tossed

flapping across the freeway
       so I'm back with my mother
              when her truck's impact flings

the deer through the windshield
       and onto her chest   slivers
              in her hands for months

and when I land I'm back
       in my father's flooded studio
              I'm ruined canvas I'm smashed plates

but if I shut my eyes   I'm safe
       in the car with my husband
              crossing the parish line at the canal

crossing the bridge   dropping
       from lit suburbs into the dark
              of drowned neighborhoods

our headlights picking shards
        from this chaos inside me
                that doesn't care where I live

The Raft of the Medusa:
after Théodore Géricault; *aux naufragés*

1. Unmooring

Step over the corpse
        and onto our raft,

                past the cameras
        and onto the raft—

wherever you step, the raft
        tilts toward you, tilts you toward

                the corpse-colored sea keeling over
        the sides, fumbling through the gaps,

swallowing its body back,
        heaving you inward: it reeks

                sliding over you, whatever you hold
        to mean *not-yet-drowned*,

the way you know the *raft*
        is snapped masts lashed too late,

                and a *mast* is a stripped tree,
        a big stick, so a broken mast goes

stick stick stick stick stick it clacks
        sidewalk-wise across picket-fence gaps

                until the raft heaves and we slide
        clinging to shit-smeared slats and thighs

—oh body made stranger than water—
    and you think you are home in the city

        which is crowds unhoused in a Dome,
  city this raft unmoored from the ship

that towed it, human weight a drag,
    adrift for days past the cameras.

2. Fever

Take my hand—you've got *phrenetis calenture*,
        heat breeds it in you sailing nowhere so long,

                fever of going nowhere, it makes
a home in your head, and you're the man

who walks off the raft into waves
        where he sees a street he knows,

                going nowhere, there, take my hand,
you're the woman lost in a house

where the sea tossed books
        and couches, where the sea broke

                walls and teacups, where the sea
drowned her dog in the attic, there,

take my hand, you're almost home,
        you're playing chess with a stranger

                in the Dome, you excuse yourself to climb
over the railing, call "move-aside-please"

to the crowded tier below, take
        my hand, before you step—

                          oh mirrors sick
        with sludge and gasoline, faces leached

from family pictures, and a ship-like speck
        that frets our horizon
                          flits away—

3. The Atelier

The painter arranges cadavers
       he will live with in his studio;

             he'll paint two rags and a stick on our horizon,
    we'll wave a red bunting, stirring the air—

Stepping back into your city, wherever
       you step the city tilts toward you

             its corpse. Blue, clear as glass,
    the sky shatters light through trees

the winds sucked and snapped, into gaps
       of charred bricks where houses burned,

             on the gravel-patched levee breach
    where a block-long barge, unmoored

in the canal, battered as the storm surged,
       battered until the waters heaved

             earth and streets aside, shattered
    home. Here's someone's purse, someone's

drowned book. Here's the barge,
       stuck in its impersonal etc.

             Oh *naufragé*, shipwrecked one,
    friend made strange by water—

The painter takes up his brush and,
       smelling dead flesh, paints it.

Motion Studies

0.

The worst part about driving in a storm
        is trusting the taillights of the bagasse truck
                crawling ten feet from your fender,

and when he exits and the clouds almost clear,
        is the next squall line hitting full on,
                its frantic body like a river undone,

and when you reach the skinny bridge
        over the bayou swollen to the embankment's lip,
                your leg aches on the accelerator, trembling,

no railing, tires troubling old wood,
        and through the wipers' feeble sweep
                no other side

1. [1929/2005]

We'll never make it in time: you're twelve,
    riding west to see a corpse in a flood,
        I'm your grandson at forty-two, riding east

to see my city's flooded remains.
    Gueydan to Port Arthur, Austin to New Orleans,
        you in a pickup with your daddy and one brother,

another brother waiting in a funeral home,
    laid out in somebody's suit on a cooling board,
        you trying to imagine that body past this rain,

me in a rental car with the music cranked,
    trying not to think about stories that got snagged
        in stories that failed to hold up, to hold

water—

A haze hangs and shifts around the border,
    starts around Orange, fades near Sulphur,
        not smoke, not mist, pale acrid miles

like the landscape's risen ghost
    hovering over snapped trees and houses
        smashed on their foundations, all broken

from the same direction: where I'm going
    while you ride listening to your daddy
        muttering *had to die in a goddam flood,*

    the truck grinding slow against mud
            and crushed shell, slurry slipping down
                      the soft bank of the swollen ditch—

Like that, the rain stops, the windshield clears
            and you can see you've gotten nowhere
                      in all that time. Another squall line—

2.

You came back from the war to your job at Texaco and bought a journal where you wrote down the only story you ever did write, the only one that mattered:

> your brother died
> > there was a flood
> > > you were too late to see him buried.

You wrote it down

and you told it to my father when he was a boy and my grandmother told it to me,

> the telling a bridge back to that crossing,

and after you died my father found the journal in your bedroom

and kept it for me in his studio:
> nine feet of lake water took it.

Somewhere in a landfill—

I'm writing this for you   is what I thought when I started this,
> now I can't tell my way out

3. [notes for a ghost claim]

November 2005:

The Pontchartrain Blvd. neutral ground, heaped half a mile some
days with dead trees uprooted, stacked two stories high,
        other days what's been gutted from houses
                siding drywall pink insulation
                        clothes stuffed animals swing sets
    every day shredded compacted hauled to the landfill

and the next day—

                                January 2006:

Walking through the lower 9th ward:

    no other side

    silence heavy as   yes   as a drowned city

    I add nothing telling what I saw: it was there

        at my feet, something shiny stuck in dried mud
        only the shock of robbing anyone's grave
            stops my hand in time

Somewhere out there, your journal—

4. [2008]

Knowing better, I go back to the newspaper's website
        and watch the animated story of the flood.
Blue arrows flash, red bursts blast—too much like dynamite—
        at each fresh breach in the levees,
and blue pours in over gray, just following the timeline.

According to Zeno, Achilles never wins. That's me
        every time I click START and the wind
makes its simulated howl and the storm never stops
        undoing—

5. [1929]

The undertaker is very sorry.
        It was too hot. The ice wouldn't keep him.
                We buried him this morning, yonder.

Y'all been driving these whole two days?
        This sure has been some flood.
                Had to wear hip boots to dig that grave.

Your father fidgets as he listens,
        twisting his hat in his hands.
                Smaller than you've ever seen him.

Already somebody else's body
        laid out where your brother's had been.
                You walk up to the cooling board

and crouch to look under the drape
        at a block of ice as big as you.
                It looks cold enough. Gray-white like his feet,

out there somewhere. Standing up, you watch
        your daddy give the undertaker cash
                and turn away, the man's grasping hand unshaken.

6.

The worst part of someone asking
    what's it like there now
        is they don't know what they're asking

has too many broken answers:
    something shiny stuck in dried mud.
        Somebody else's body.

A tortoise nosing out a grub.
    Smear of paint, rice powder, words—
        knowing better, I came home.

Barton Springs

September, 2005

Darling, our city's destroyed and here we are,
        trying to relax at this chilly Texas pool,
                sole habitat of a red-gilled salamander nearly extinct.

From the ledge, I watch you scissor-kick across
        until you bump into another friend from home.
                You stop to chat, exchanging news, I know,

about whose studio the flood wiped out,
        whose mother hasn't turned up anywhere,
                who saw a body floating in a canal,

who slogged through his house to find
        photographs on the floor, the frames intact,
                the images blank, dissolved by the same muck

that sucked the words out of books,
        left a sludge of loved ones' faces,
                ruined stories. A crawfish crawls

along the stone ledge. It's a native,
        apparently; it's right at home. Last night,
                I cleaned the stove in our new apartment,

crying, then watered the drought-dead lawn,
        crying, then drank on the back porch, tired,
                my darling, my salamander, of crying—

I take a breath, kick off from the ledge,
        and swim out, past extinction,
                to touch.

NOTES

The epigraphs to "From the Dark Chamber" are from *Secrets of the Dark Chamber: The Art of the American Dageurreotype*, ed. Foresta, Merry and John Wood, the catalogue of an exhibition at the National Museum of American Art (Smithsonian Institute Press, 1995).

The first "Motion Studies" series draws on many sources, including, for claims concerning the death of Zeno of Elea, *Documents for the Study of the Gospels*, ed. Cartlidge, David and David Dungan (Fortress Press, 1980).

In "The Cooling Board," the last poem in the second "Motion Studies" series, "Spindletop" refers to a major oil strike near Beaumont, Texas. On January 10, 1901, after years of exploration and drilling at the Spindletop Hill salt dome, a gusher blew 150 feet in the air, and continued spewing at the rate of 100,000 barrels per day before it was capped.

One line in "Eakins Odalisque" is amended from the title of an essay by Elizabeth Johns, "An Avowal of Artistic Community: Nudity and Fantasy in Thomas Eakins' Photographs" (in *Eakins and the Photograph*, Smithsonian Institute Press/Pennsylvania Academy of the Fine Arts, 1994).

In "Three Essays on *Swimming*," one line in "Is it democratic?" is borrowed from Richard R. Brettell's essay "Thomas Eakins and the Male Nude in French Vanguard Painting, 1850-1890," in *Thomas Eakins and the Swimming Picture*, ed. Bolger, Doreen and Sarah Cash (Amon Carter Museum, Fort Worth, TX, 1996). The Whitman material in the last section of "Is it democratic?" comes from "Specimen Days" and other texts.

The epigraph to "Susan Macdowell Eakins at the Memorial Exhibition of Her Husband's Work" is quoted in Henry Adams' *Eakins Revealed*. The opening lines of the last section are from a letter by SME, quoted in "In Search of True Tones," Mark Tucker and Nica Gutman (in *Thomas Eakins*, exhibition catalogue, Philadelphia Museum of Art, 2001).

The interactive flood map mentioned in section 4 of the third "Motion Studies" series can be found at http://www.nola.com/katrina/wide.ssf?/katrina/graphics/flashflood.swf.

VISITING THE 2002 RETROSPECTIVE of Thomas Eakins' work at the Metropolitan Museum, I came to *Swimming*. I detested it. I loved it. I wanted it to mean something other than what it was, but what it simply was—in its abstract composition, its rendering of time and naked forms—kept drawing me back to it. Back home in New Orleans, I began reading about it. The next summer, I spent three days at the Amon Carter Museum in Fort Worth studying it. Overwhelmed, I began writing my way into it.

I found, in *Swimming* and other works, compelling ambiguities that made me think about the body, time (as history, as lived moment, as motion), desire, Whitman. My poems express a fraction of my complicated response to Eakins and his work. I take the word "essay" in the sense that Montaigne meant it: as an attempt.

—BRAD RICHARD

Thomas Eakins, American, 1844-1916, *Swimming*, 1885, oil on canvas, 27 3/8 x 36 3/8 inches. Amon Carter Museum, Fort Worth, Texas. Purchased by the Friends of Art, Fort Worth Art Association, 1925; acquired by the Amon Carter Museum, 1990, from the Modern Art Museum of Fort Worth through grants and donations from the Amon G. Carter Foundation, the Sid W. Richardson Foundation, the Anne Burnett and Charles Tandy Foundation, Capital Cities/ABC Foundation, Fort Worth Star-Telegram, The R. D. and Joan Dale Hubbard Foundation, and the people of Fort Worth.

ABOUT THE AUTHOR

Brad Richard is chair of the creative writing program at Lusher Charter High School in New Orleans. A native of Texas and Louisiana, he received his B.A. from the University of Iowa and his M.F.A. from Washington University in St. Louis. His first book of poems, *Habitations* (Portals Press, 2000), was followed by the chapbook, *The Men in the Dark* (Lowlands Press, 2004). Richard is the 2002 Winner in the Poets & Writers, Inc., Writers Exchange competition, and his work has appeared in a wide range of journals, including *American Letters & Commentary*, *Bayou*, *Hunger Mountain*, *The Iowa Review*, *Literary Imagination*, *Prairie Schooner*, *The Massachusetts Review*, *North American Review*, *Passages North*, and *Witness*.

ABOUT THE WASHINGTON PRIZE

Motion Studies is the winner of the 2010 Word Works Washington Prize. Brad Richard's collection was selected from among 204 manuscripts submitted in February by American and Canadian poets.

FIRST READERS: Stuart Bartow • Pete Borrebach • George Drew
Peter Fernbach • Michelle Galo • Elaine Handley • Amanda Hosey
Diane Lockward • Marilyn McCabe • Kathleen McCoy
Mary Sanders Shartle • David Svenson

SECOND READERS: Carrie Bennett • Allen Hoey • Jay Rogoff
Barbara Ungar

FINAL JUDGES: Karren Alenier • J. H. Beall • Margo Stever
Nancy White • Maria van Beuren

OTHER WASHINGTON PRIZE BOOKS

Nathalie F. Anderson, *Following Fred Astaire*, 1998
Michael Atkinson, *One Hundred Children Waiting for a Train*, 2001
Carrie Bennett, *biography of water*, 2004
Peter Blair, *Last Heat*, 1999
Richard Carr, *Ace*, 2008
Ann Rae Jonas, *A Diamond Is Hard But Not Tough*, 1997
Frannie Lindsay, *Mayweed*, 2009
Richard Lyons, *Fleur Carnivore*, 2005
Fred Marchant, *Tipping Point*, 1993, 3rd printing 1999
Ron Mohring, *Survivable World*, 2003
Brad Richard, *Motion Studies*, 2010
Jay Rogoff, *The Cutoff*, 1994
Prartho Sereno, *Call from Paris*, 2007
Enid Shomer, *Stalking the Florida Panther*, 1987, 2nd printing 1993
John Surowiecki, *The Hat City after Men Stopped Wearing Hats*, 2006
Miles Waggener, *Phoenix Suites*, 2002
Nancy White, *Sun, Moon, Salt*, 1992, 2nd edition 2010

ABOUT THE WORD WORKS

The Word Works, a nonprofit literary organization, publishes contemporary poetry in fine editions. Since 1981, it has sponsored the Washington Prize, a $1,500 award to an American or Canadian poet. Monthly since 1999, The Word Works has presented free literary programs in the Chevy Chase, MD, Café Muse series, and each summer, free poetry programs are held at the historic Joaquin Miller Cabin in Washington, DC's Rock Creek Park. Every year, two high school students debut in the Miller Cabin Series as winners of the Jacklyn Potter Young Poets Competition.

Since 1974, Word Works programs have included: "In the Shadow of the Capitol," a symposium and archival project on the African American intellectual community in segregated Washington, DC; the Gunston Arts Center Poetry Series (Ai, Carolyn Forché, and Stanley Kunitz, among others); the Poet Editor panel discussions at The Writer's Center (John Hollander, Maurice English, Anthony Hecht, Josephine Jacobsen, and others); and Master Class workshops (Agha Shahid Ali, Thomas Lux, Marilyn Nelson).

In 2011, The Word Works will have published 73 titles, including work from such authors as Deirdra Baldwin, Christopher Bursk, Barbara Goldberg, Edward Weismiller, and Mac Wellman. Currently, The Word Works publishes books and occasional anthologies under three imprints: the Washington Prize, the Hilary Tham Capital Collection, and International Editions.

As a 501(c)3 organization, The Word Works has received awards from the National Endowment for the Arts, National Endowment for the Humanities, DC Commission on the Arts & Humanities, Witter Bynner Foundation, The Writer's Center, Bell Atlantic, Batir Foundation, the David G. Taft Foundation, and others, including many generous private patrons. The Word Works has established an archive of artistic and administrative materials in the Washington Writers Archive housed in the George Washington University Gelman Library.

Please enclose a self-addressed, stamped envelope with all inquiries.

The Word Works
PO Box 42164
Washington, DC 20015

wordworksbooks.org
editor@wordworksbooks.org

OTHER AVAILABLE WORD WORKS BOOKS

From the Hilary Tham Capital Collection

Mel Belin, *Flesh That Was Chrysalis*
Doris Brody, *Judging the Distance*
Sarah Browning, *Whiskey in the Garden of Eden*
Christopher Conlon, *Gilbert and Garbo in Love*
    Mary Falls: Requiem for Mrs. Surratt
Donna Denizé, *Broken Like Job*
W. Perry Epes, *Nothing Happened*
James Hopkins, *Eight Pale Women*
Brandon Johnson, *Love's Skin*
Judith McCombs, *The Habit of Fire*
Miles David Moore, *The Bears of Paris*
    Rollercoaster
Kathi Morrison-Taylor, *By the Nest*
Maria Terrone, *The Bodies We Were Loaned*
Hilary Tham, *Bad Names for Women*
    Counting
Barbara Ungar, *Charlotte Brontë, You Ruined My Life*
Jonathan Vaile, *Blue Cowboy*
Rosemary Winslow, *Green Bodies*
Michele Wolf, *Immersion*

International Editions

Yoko Danno & James C. Hopkins, *The Blue Door*
Moshe Dor, Barbara Goldberg, Giora Leshem, eds., *The Stones Remember*
Myong-Hee Kim, *Crow's Eye View: The Infamy of Lee Sang, Korean Poet*
Vladimir Levchev, *Black Book of the Endangered Species*

Additional Titles

Karren L. Alenier, Hilary Tham, Miles David Moore, eds.,
    Winners: A Retrospective of the Washington Prize
Jacklyn Potter, Dwaine Rieves, Gary Stein, eds.,
    Cabin Fever: Poets at Joaquin Miller's Cabin
Robert Sargent, *Aspects of a Southern Story*
    A Woman From Memphis

www.ingramcontent.com/pod-product-compliance
Lightning Source LLC
Chambersburg PA
CBHW031207090426
42736CB00009B/823